12 Interpretations for Piano

Arranged by Antonio Ciacca

Published by TwinsMusic Enterprises Corporation
Project manager: Giusy Magri
Cover Photo by Andrea Palmucci
Biography Photo by Lorenza Cerbini
Proof Reading by Lucio Ferrara
Design by Nick Finzer and Outside in Music

Copyright © 2014 TwinsMusic Enterprises Corporation
All Rights Reserved
ISBN: 978-0-9828249-8-6

www.twinsmusic.it
www.nyjazzcworkshop.com

No part of this publication may be reproduced, stored in retrieval
system, or transmitted, in any form or by any means electronic,
mechanical, photocopying, recording, or otherwise without
prior consent of Antonio Ciacca and TwinsMusic Enterprises
Corporation.

Contents

BEAUTIFUL LOVE by Victor Young 4

BUT NOT FOR ME by George Gershwin 7

DANY MY DEAR by Antonio Ciacca 10

FOR ALL WE KNOW by S. Lewis, F. Cots 12

I HEAR A RHAPSODY by G. Fragos, J. Backer, D. Gasparre 14

DANY MY DEAR Lyrics by Antonio Ciacca and Justin Echols 17

IN A SENTIMENTAL MOOD by Duke Ellington 18

IT COULD HAPPEN TO YOU by Burke, VanHeusen 22

POLKADOTS AND MOONBEAMS by Jimmy VanHeusen 25

PRELUDE TO A KISS by Duke Ellington 28

STARDUST by Hoagy Carmichael 31

WILLOW WEEP FOR ME by Ann Ronnell 34

YOU DO SOMETHING TO ME by Cole Porter 37

Beautiful Love

By Victor Young

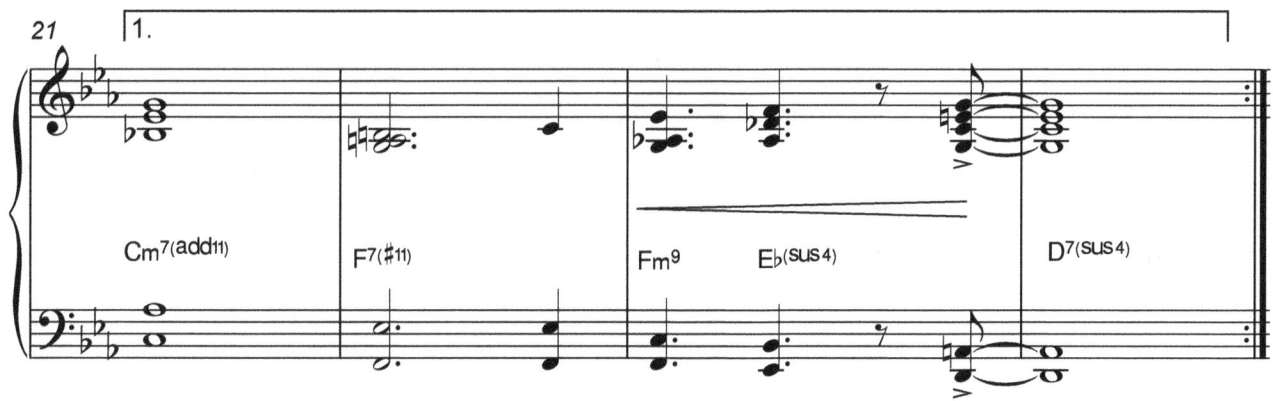
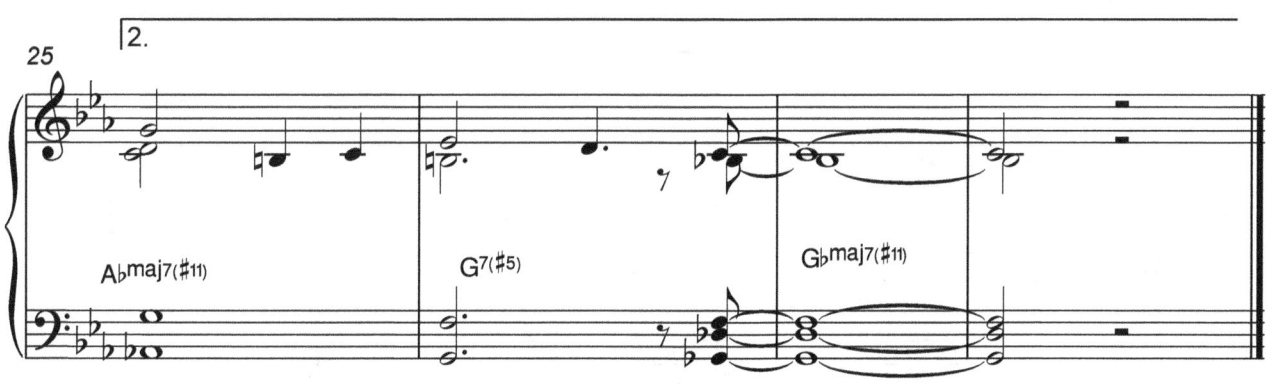

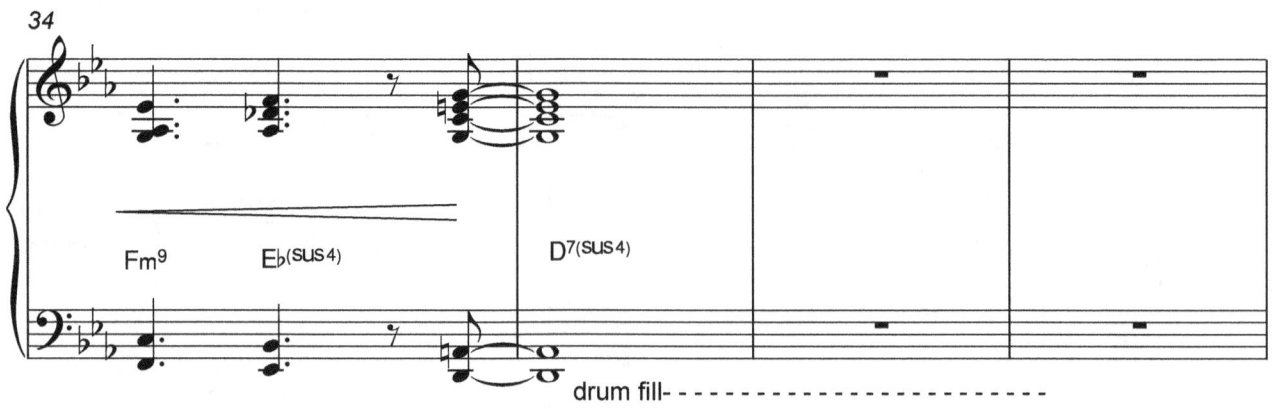
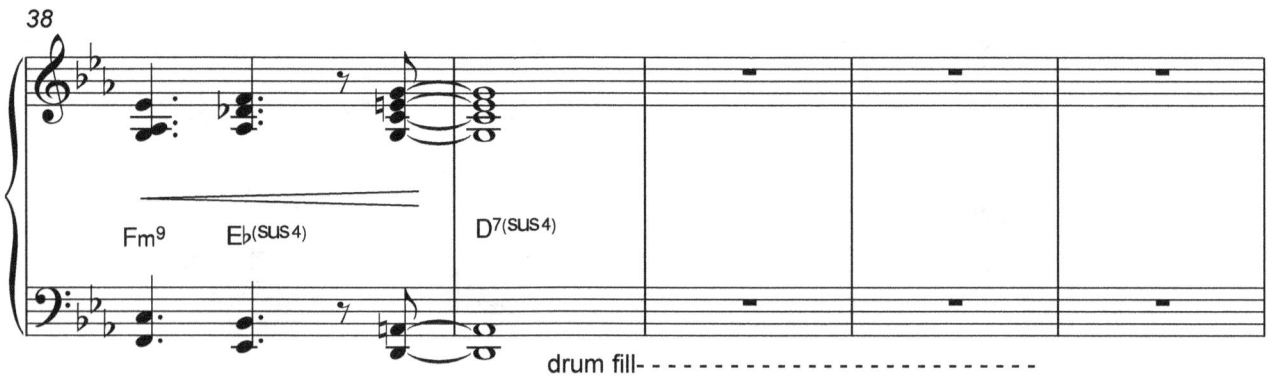
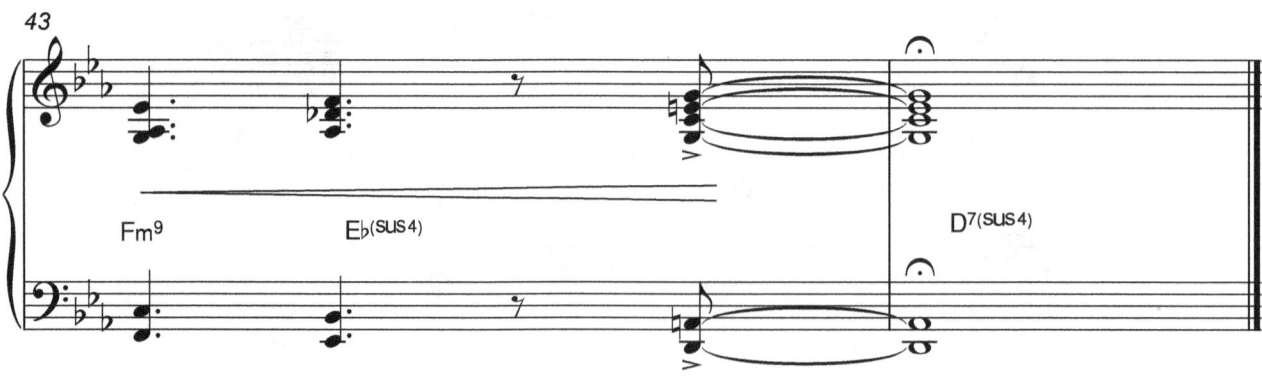

But Not for Me

By George Gershwin

7

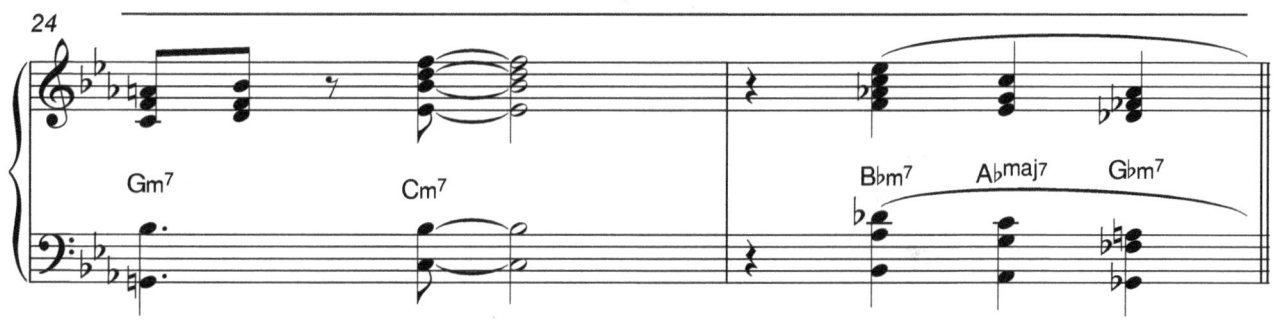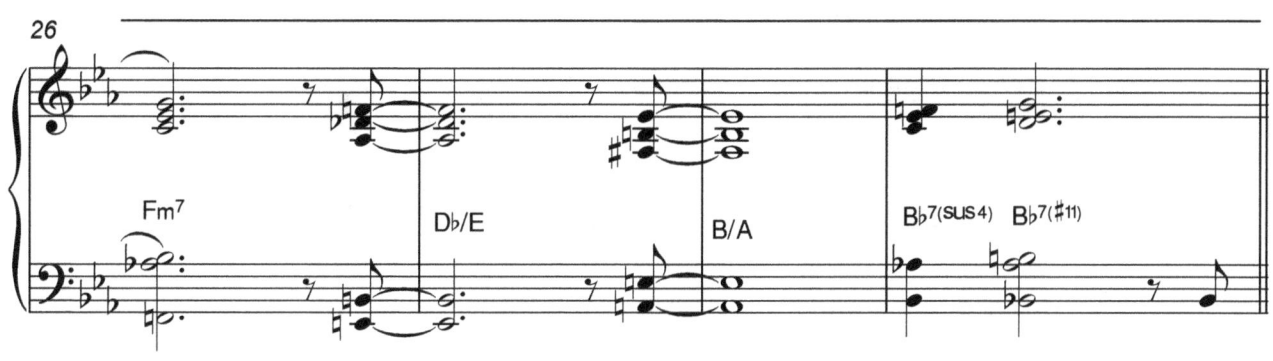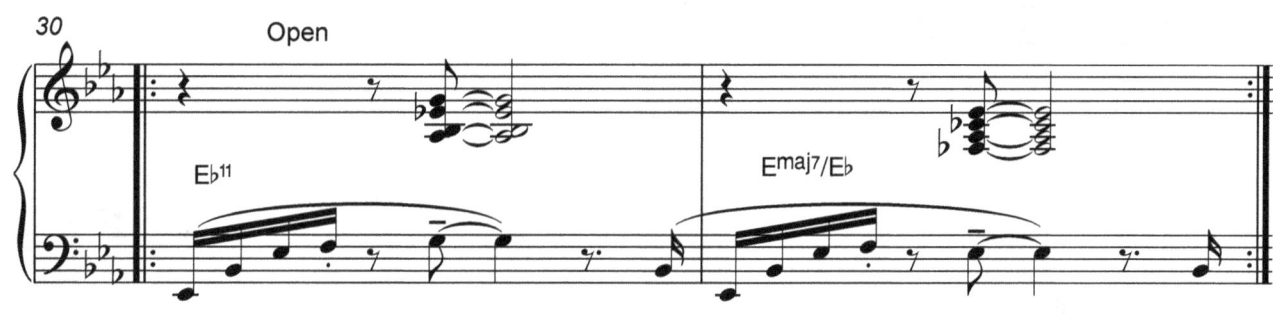

Dany My Dear

By Antonio Ciacca

For All We Know

By S.Lewis and F. Cots.

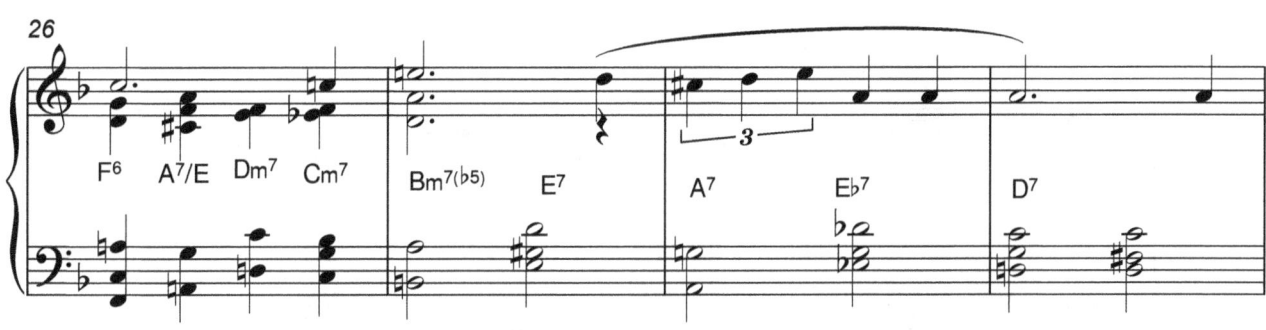

I Hear a Rhapsody

G.Fragos-J.Backer-D.Gasparre

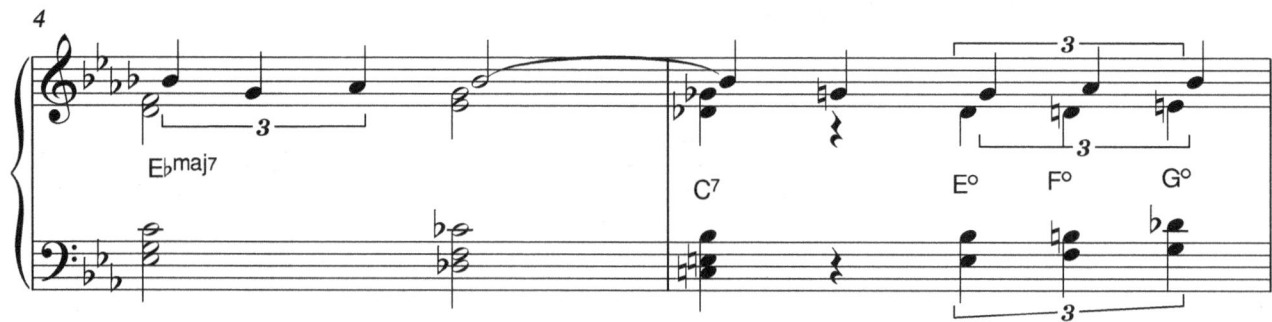

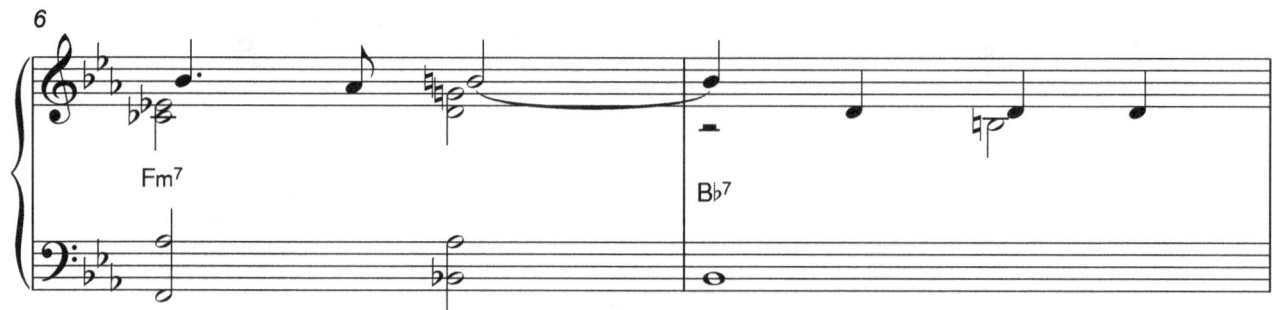

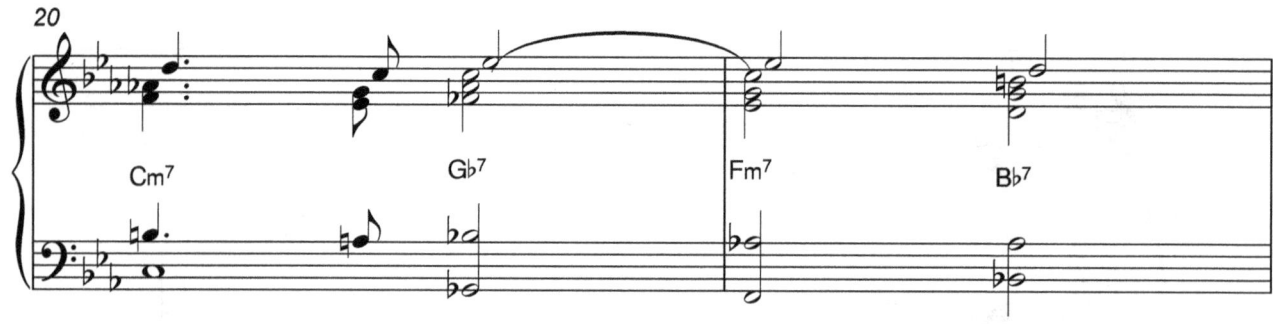
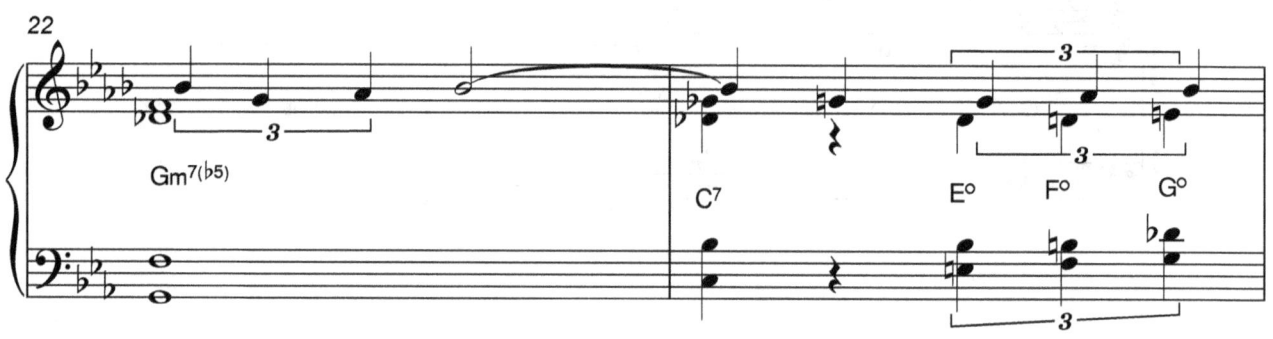
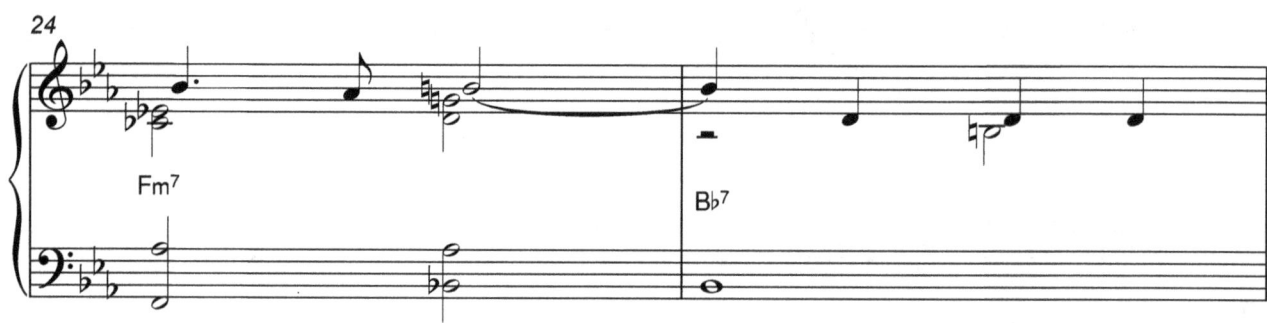
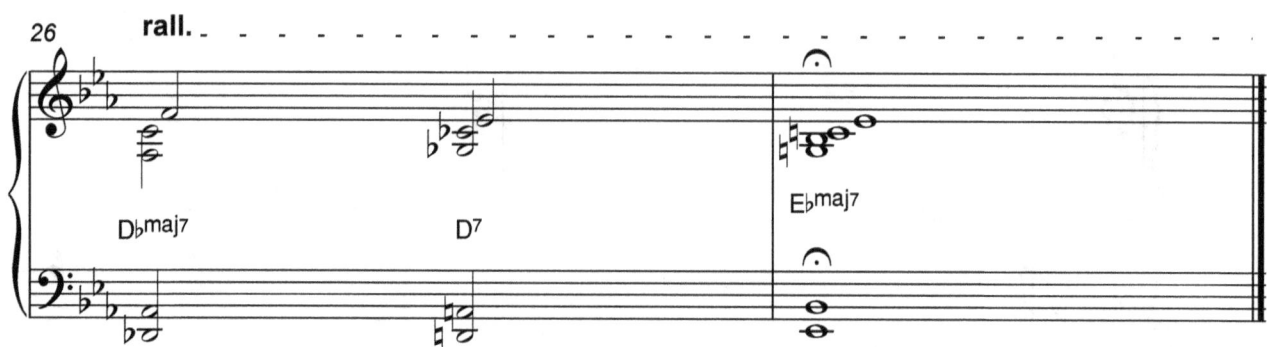

Dany My Dear

Lyrics by Antonio Ciacca and Justin Echols

Chase your dream
Though it seems
Life it may never give you
All that you wished it'd bring you Dany.

Share your dreams
When it seems
Those who you give yourself to
Aren't prepared to receive you Dany.

You are the shining sun
You are the precious one
All that you do will prosper
If you all that you have you offer.

Now you gleam
And it seems
All of the world they knew you
Chased your dreams.

In a Sentimental Mood

by Duke Ellington

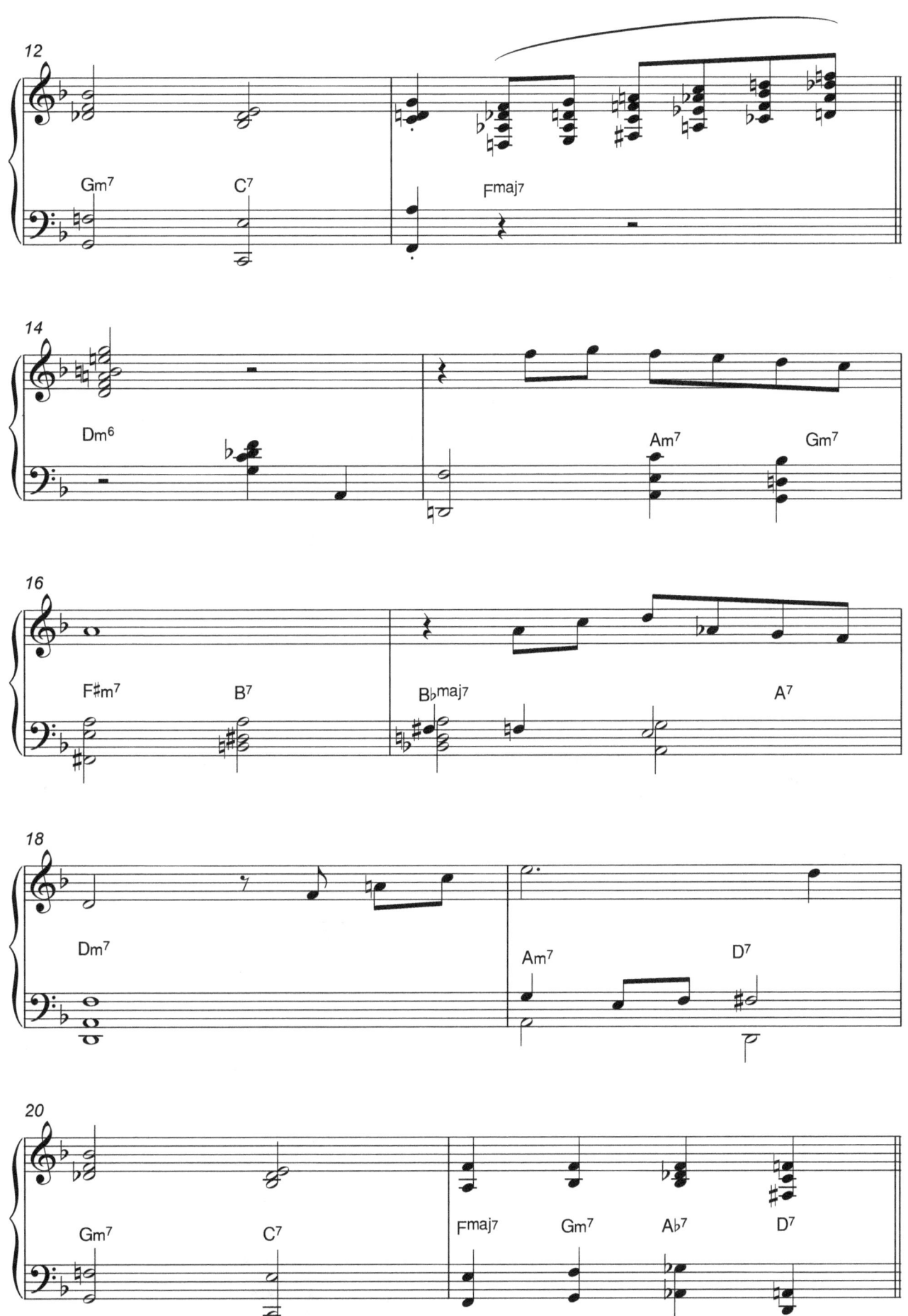

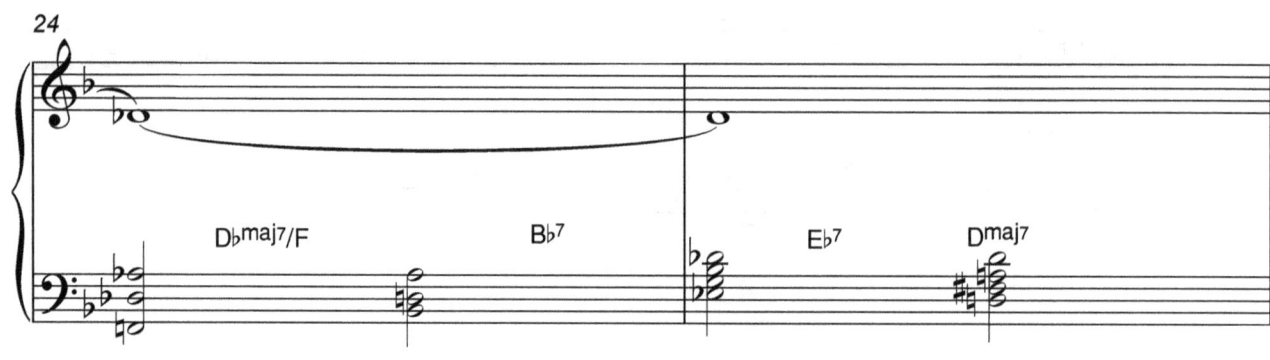

It Could Happen to You

by Burke-Van Heusen

Polkadots and Moonbeams

By Jimmy Van Heusen

Prelude to a Kiss

By Duke Ellington

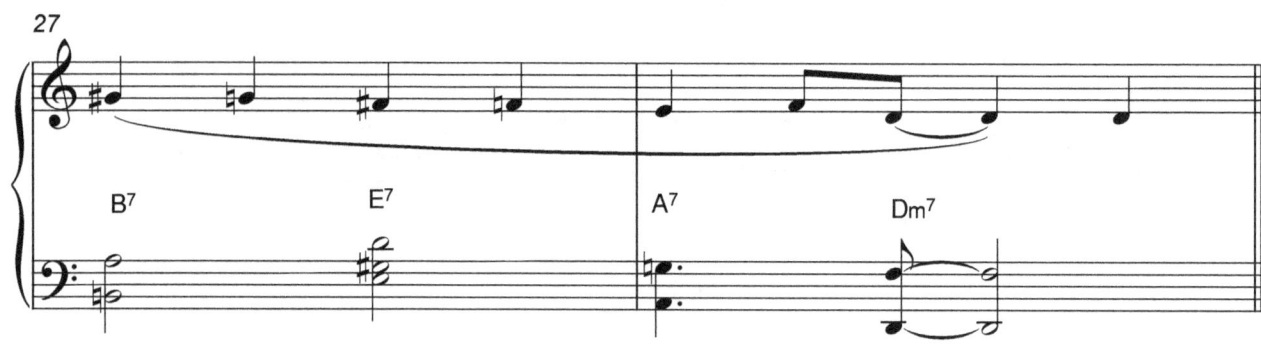

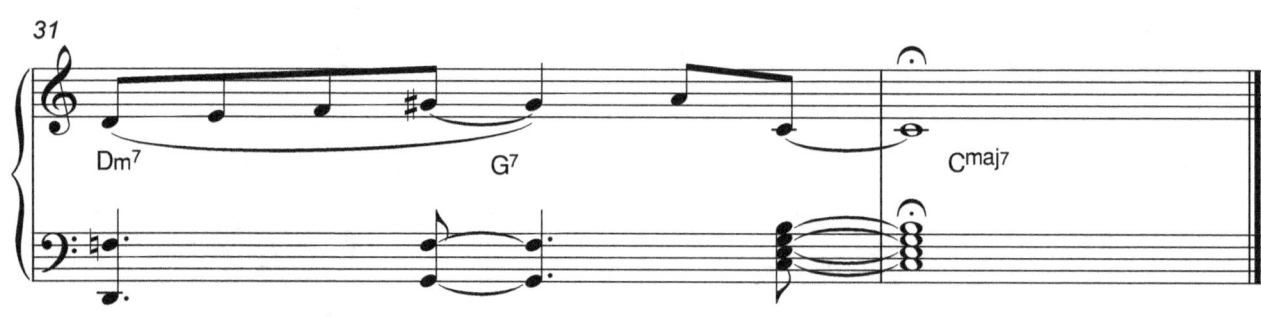

Stardust

By Hoagy Carmichael

31

Willow Weep for Me

By Ann Ronnell

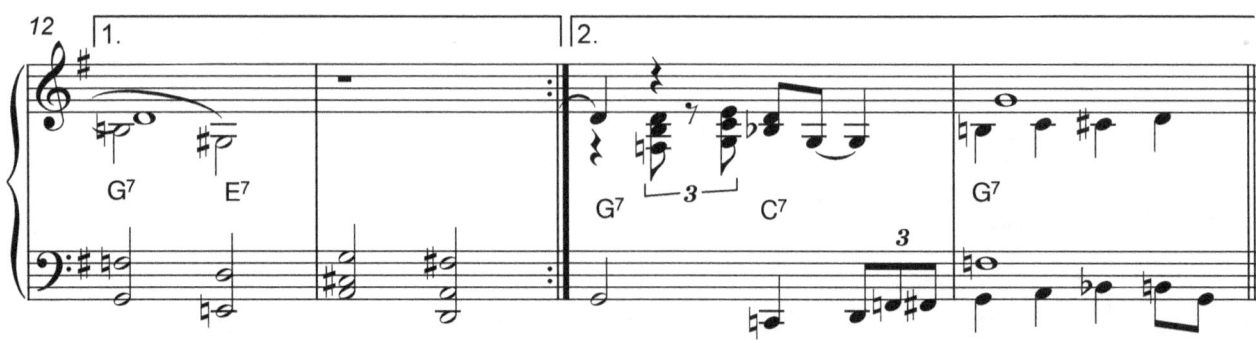

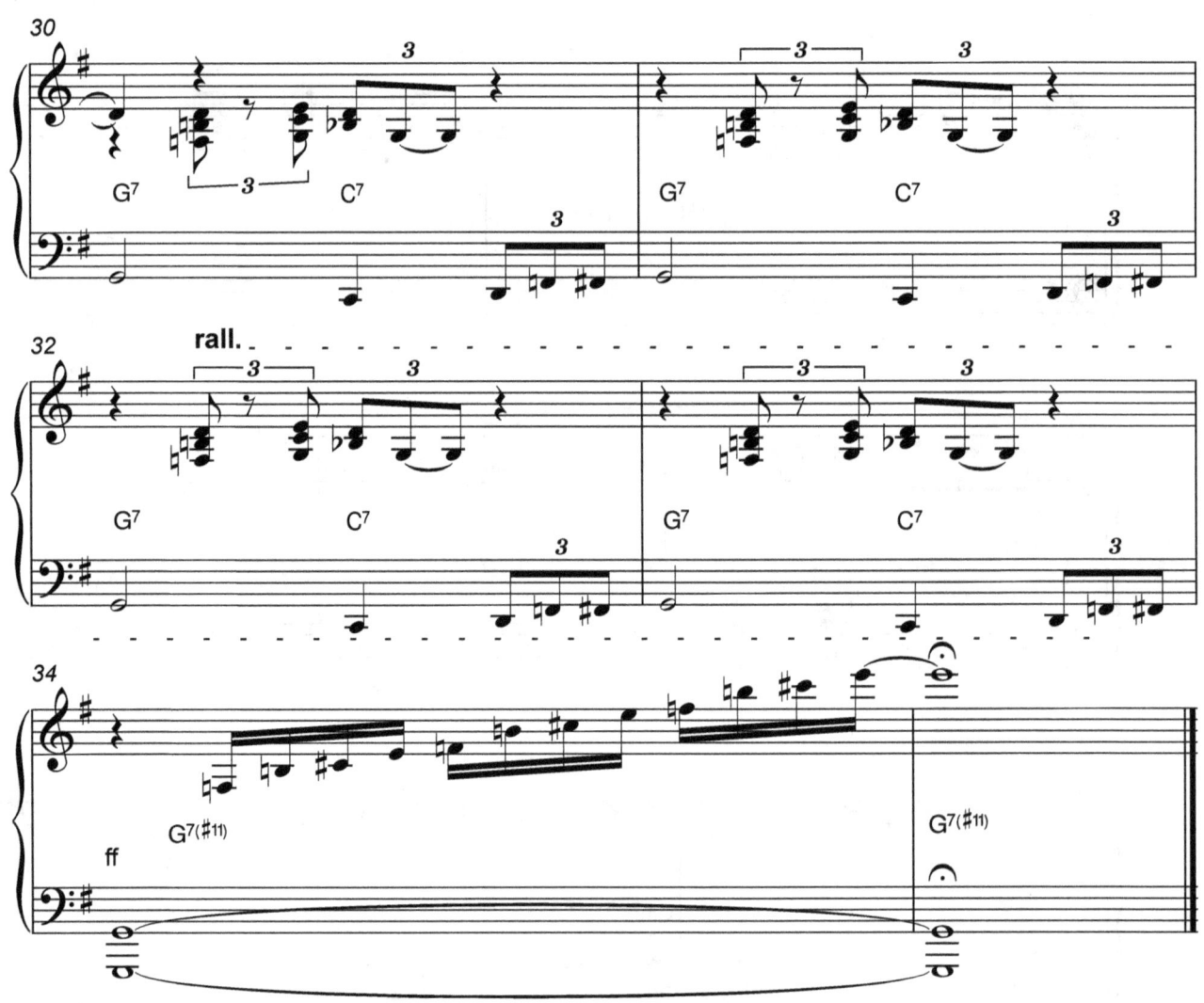

You Do Something to Me

By Cole Porter

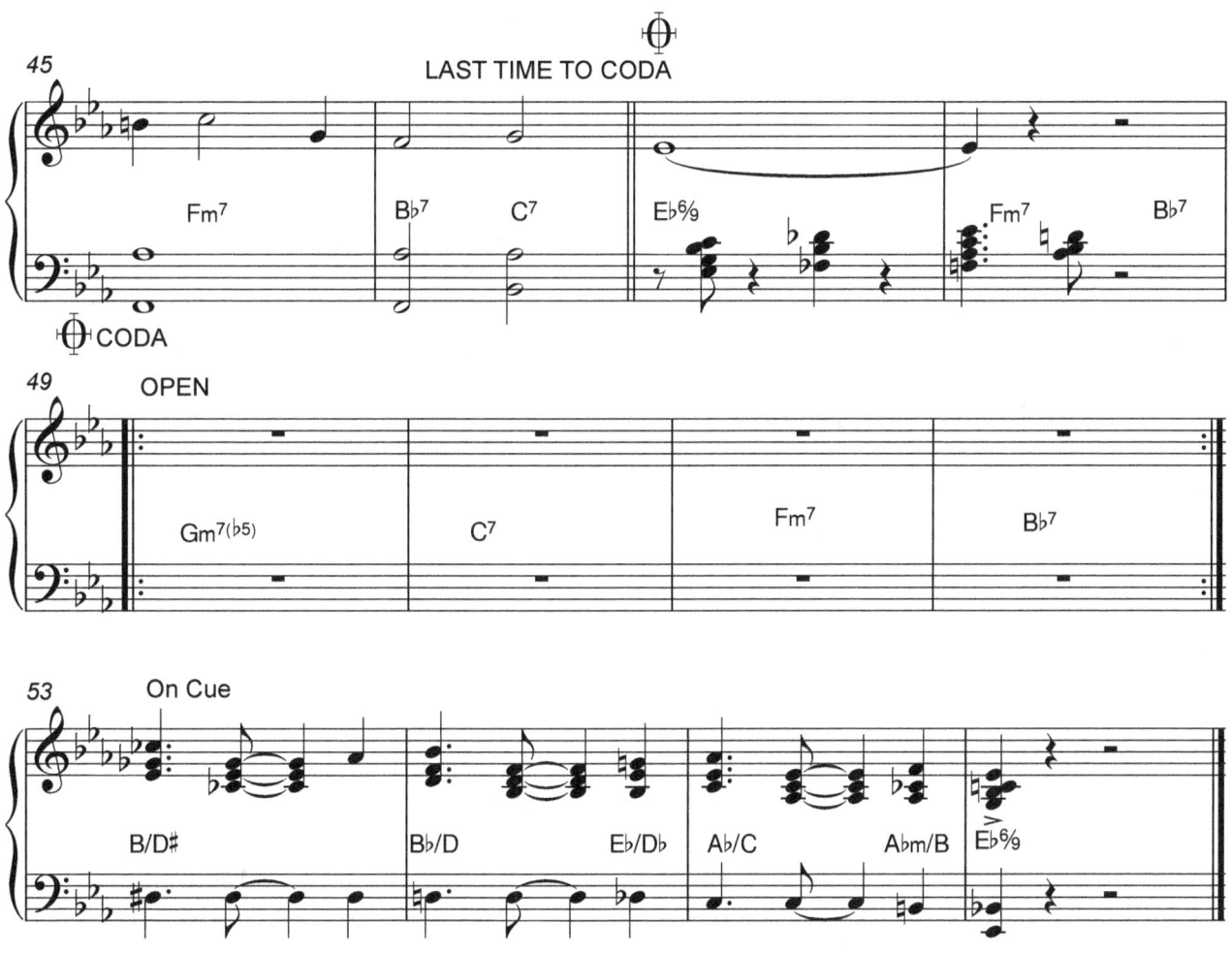

About Antonio Ciacca:

Born in Germany, raised in Italy and educated in the United States, pianist, composer, and arts administrator Antonio Ciacca has established himself as an indomitable artist, consummate musician, and powerful advocate of the jazz tradition.

Ciacca began his career as a sideman for such acclaimed jazz artists as Art Farmer, James Moody, Lee Konitz, Jonny Griffin, Mark Murphy, Dave Liebman, and Steve Grossman. It was Grossman's influence—with whom he studied for three years beginning in 1990—that particularly nurtured Ciacca's own development. In 1993, Ciacca moved to Detroit to study at Wayne State University with Kenny Barron, after which he studied privately with Jackie Byard in New York. Whilst living in Detroit, he was first exposed to gospel music, an influence he soon integrated it into his own developing style as a composer and performer; Ciacca eventually went on to produce a CD for the Detroit Gospel Singers.

1997 proved a watershed year for Ciacca, as legendary saxophonist Steve Lacy invited Ciacca to join his quartet, a collaboration that would last for seven years. The same year, Antonio Ciacca met Wynton Marsalis, who was performing in Italy with Elvin Jones. This meeting laid the foundation for a friendship and musical collaboration that continued through their work together at Jazz at Lincoln Center. The following year, Ciacca began performing with saxophonist Benny Golson, with whom he continues to collaborate.

In 2007, Ciacca's extensive music industry experience and comprehensive artistic vision led to his being tapped to take on the position of Director of Programming at Jazz at Lincoln Center, a role he held until 2011. Ciacca has expanded his role into new entrepreneurial ventures to promote his music. Establishing himself as the Artist in Resident at New York City's Setai Hotel, he has curated one of the most exciting nightly jazz series in New York, and has partnered the venue in unique musical events, including the "Remembering Bud" Jazz Festival and Italian Jazz Days.

Throughout his career, Ciacca has served as a tireless jazz advocate and educator, and in 2009 expanded this role as he began teaching "Business of Jazz" at the esteemed Juilliard School of Music in New York. In addition to teaching at Juilliard, Ciacca is an active lecturer throughout the United States and Europe, conducting numerous workshops on jazz business, on piano technique, and on ensemble work.

As a bandleader, Ciacca's work is documented in six highly acclaimed solo albums. His debut album, Driemoty, was released on the C-Jam label in 1995. Most recently, Ciacca has formed a close relationship with the American label Motema, for whom he has recorded two albums: Rush Life in 2008 and Lagos Blues—featuring Ciacca's mentor Steve Grossman—in 2010. Ciacca's skills as a vital composer are also documented in music books: The Music of Antonio Ciacca, Vol. 1, as well as the companion books to Driemoty and to Lagos Blues. Additionally Antonio has made his debut appearance at Carnegie Hall as pianist, composer and arranger for the New York Pops.